Affil.

The Methodology Of Generating Income Through
Affiliate Marketing Via Youtube Product Reviews And
Utilizing The Amazon Associates Program

*(The Most Straightforward Path For Novices To Generate
Income Through Affiliate Marketing)*

Reginald Hopkins

TABLE OF CONTENT

Picking A Product

Clickbank offers an extensive range of products, particularly within the evergreen niches. It is recommended to select a product that closely aligns with your specific niche and relevant keywords. The more specific and targeted it is the better it will convert, so again if your niche / keyword is 'dating for men over 50' then find one similar to that instead

If feasible, in the context of a comprehensive dating manual. Clickbank provides comprehensive tutorials on

In relation to all subjects, you can effortlessly discover something highly relevant to your specific keywords and niche. Typically, my approach involves initially identifying a specific market segment and conducting comprehensive keyword research, after which I proceed to carefully evaluate and choose a suitable Clickbank product.

DOMAIN NAME

After selecting your niche, finalizing your keyword, and devising a profitable strategy, you may proceed with establishing your website. This section is expeditious and straightforward. Initially, it is advisable to proceed with the registration of a domain.

Register A Domain

I choose to utilize NameCheap as my domain registrar due to my favorable experience with their user-friendly website and registration process, as well as their established reputation for dependability and competitive pricing. If Name Cheap does not meet your requirements, Go Daddy can be considered as an alternative.

Picking A Domain

The majority of the guidance available on mini niche sites suggests utilizing exact match domains (EMDs), which essentially means incorporating your keyword into your URL. However, I would like to deviate from this recommendation for the following system. I have expressed my belief for quite some time now that EMDs will eventually face penalties from Google, and on September 29, 2012, this prediction came true, as it is commonly regarded as an indication of a site with subpar quality. It is evident that not all EMD sites exhibit low quality, and it is not to suggest that every site will face consequences; however, it is advisable to refrain from providing Google with any grounds to single out your site. Therefore, it is recommended to opt for a URL that is more general or generic, without the inclusion of your keyword.

In the case of a website targeting the keyword "supplements for insomnia," alternatives in a formal register could be insomniaHQ.com, insomniainfo.net, or sleepeasy.com. These domain names possess an authoritative appeal, even resembling established brands. The specific choice you make bears little significance, as long as it aligns with your niche. Therefore, it is unnecessary to expend excessive time and energy brainstorming for attention-grabbing names.

Which domain extension should I choose, .com or .net?

A top preference for me would invariably be a dot com, succeeded by a dot net. If that is not feasible, I would contemplate opting for a .org or a .info domain; however, it should be noted that they do not possess the same level of credibility. Make an effort to locate a dot com whenever feasible and refrain from using an exact match domain (EMD) or Google alternative.
There is a possibility that you may be subject to consequences for producing work of substandard quality.

Additional Domain Options

After identifying an appropriate domain, proceed to complete the registration process. Frequently, you will be presented with a multitude of additional services that are available for purchase in conjunction with your domain, such as web hosting, branded email, and privacy enhancements. The sole option I opt for is the 'whois' privacy options (which are provided free of charge for the initial year through NameCheap). The remaining choices hold no significance to me, and I consistently endorse this particular option.

Acquiring hosting and email services from distinct entities is preferable, as any issues concerning the domain or hosting would result in significant complications if both were managed by a single entity.

How to locate a suitable affiliate program.

Pursue a Suitable Program Based on Your Prior Experiences

Therefore, it has been ascertained that it is imperative to possess unwavering belief in the product being endorsed in order to achieve success in one's affiliate marketing pursuits. Therefore, we will commence our search here to identify a program that will be your initial choice for promotion.

Please retrieve a piece of paper or access a Word document and commence the process of recording your areas of interest. Jot down your hobbies. Your skills. Your areas of expertise. It may pertain to one's professional endeavors or be unrelated to their professional pursuits.

Should you have young children, perhaps consider documenting notable toy brands and embarking on a blog dedicated to toy evaluations. Toys will subsequently qualify as a deductible business expense, enabling you to obtain a tax deduction for purchasing toys for your children.

Same goes for electronics. If you like computers, start a computer review blog and computers and equipment will become a write-off.

Alternatively, should you desire to procure desirable items for your spouse, consider establishing a discerning review blog pertaining to their preferences. Subsequently, it would be permissible for you to utilize the gains of your business venture to make purchases on their behalf.

Moreover, it is not solely centered on the acquisition of material possessions. You are required to compile a comprehensive repertoire of factors that will sustain your interest in the long term, while simultaneously possessing the capacity to generate sustainable financial returns for your business by capitalizing on their substantial market demand.

Compile a comprehensive roster of companies or sectors presently, and subsequently, within this chapter, we will delve into the methodologies of leveraging this compilation to identify exceptional affiliate opportunities within your specific industry.

Where is the money presently located?
One aspect that requires investigation is determining the locations where fervent supporters are currently investing their income.

If individuals are making expenditures within a particular niche, it does not necessarily indicate that the market is saturated with excessive competition, and thus, one should not refrain from venturing into that domain.

What this implies is that individuals are facing a challenge which this particular domain is addressing, and are already allocating funds to resolve their predicament. You simply need to discover the means by which to access that source of revenue by leveraging your distinctive value proposition.

Later in the book, we will delve into the topic of bonus offers. However, it is important to note at this point that individuals have the ability to augment existing products by incorporating their own content and bonuses. This strategic approach has the potential to enhance the desirability of these products, thereby motivating individuals to purchase them through your affiliated link.

"When considering the whereabouts of the funds, it is highly likely that they are already accounted for in the aforementioned list compiled in the preceding section." You have compiled a catalogue of items that bring you joy, and it is probable that you have allocated financial resources towards acquiring these items. It is highly likely that you are not the sole individual in this particular circumstance. If the interests you have documented are extremely specialized, and you are aware that your target audience will be limited in size, it might be prudent to reconsider the affiliate offers you intend to pursue, or to slightly expand the scope of your interest category.

One possible illustration could be your affinity for engaging in the tabletop game called "The 13th Age," notwithstanding the limited scope of its market. Perhaps you wish to expand your interests to encompass the entirety of tabletop role-playing games.

Perhaps you possess a deep affinity for fly fishing; however, it is worth considering that a more diversified fishing affiliate venture would effectively reach a wider demographic.

While it is advisable to avoid targeting a overly narrow market, it remains essential to impart a distinct and innovative perspective in order to establish a distinctive brand and emerge as a frontrunner in your respective industry. This phenomenon is often referred to by marketers as the identification of a novel market space.

In essence, we are presenting remedies to challenges that arise within our marine ecosystem, whereupon the consumption of fish by sharks (as consumers) causes the ocean to assume a crimson hue. It's overcrowded and busy. We must endeavor to identify and capitalize on an exceptional product or innovative solution that sets us apart, and ensure its widespread exposure.

Find where the money is going and build a better or faster solution, and you will redirect the money to yourself by helping people.

That encapsulates the core essence of affiliate marketing.

Joining A Marketplace

Although it is feasible to participate in an affiliate program offered by a solitary enterprise, it is highly probable that you will eventually delving into affiliate marketplaces.

The inception of my initial marketplace occurred when we commenced the promotion of Noom. Their program was developed using the Impact Radius platform, which is currently referred to as Impact. We established a strategic partnership with Noom, wherein Impact assumed responsibility for tracking sales on behalf of the company and managing the collection and disbursement of payments.

Shortly after enrolling in the Noom program, I discovered the opportunity to participate in the Impact Marketplace, which facilitated access to other brands' programs for potential application.

At Impact, there is a strict prohibition on endorsing any arbitrary brand encountered on the platform. You are required to actively seek out opportunities relevant to your specialization, complete a concise application, and subsequently allow businesses the opportunity to assess your suitability for their program by reviewing your profile.

It can be likened to perusing various partnerships in a manner similar to window-shopping, with the added advantage of being able to promptly submit applications. Marketplaces have the potential to greatly facilitate the lives of affiliate marketers. "You have the opportunity to submit an application for membership in the esteemed Impact Marketplace at

marketplace looks like:

In recent times, they have initiated the inclusion of Pre-Qualified brands, thereby simplifying the process to a mere application for entry. This is a beneficial supplementary feature that enables you to quickly commence the promotion of an affiliate offer.

However, not all marketplaces adhere to this approach, which requires obtaining authorization from every individual brand. Certain platforms, such as Brandcycle, require prospective users to undergo an application process for acceptance into their marketplace. However, once admitted, one gains the ability to promote offers from any brand that consents to participate within said marketplace.

This creates an opportunity for a broader range of promotional offers from various companies. BrandCycle offers a diverse selection of retail establishments spanning various categories, making it a viable choice for individuals seeking to sell tangible merchandise such as apparel and toys. You have the option to submit an application to Brandcycle at

BrandCycle offers a wide array of brand options, which can be observed in this thorough list organized in alphabetical order: "

I have been informed about another marketplace named Clickbank, although I have not personally utilized it. They possess an extensive array of promotional opportunities, encompassing software and courses in various categories such as E-business, families, games, and additional areas. They possess a vast array of over 4,000 products and offer commission rates that can rise as high as 90%. You have the opportunity to personally inspect and evaluate that particular item at your own discretion.

If you seek additional promotional opportunities that align with your specific industry, or if you are uncertain about how to commence, enlisting in a marketplace presents an excellent point of origin. Please exercise caution to avoid excessively endorsing multiple items simultaneously.

Engage in the sale of products from the Amazon marketplace.

If you have a genuine interest in pursuing affiliate marketing on Amazon, I am prepared to provide you with a comprehensive overview. However, it is important to bear in mind that my observations regarding this program have not yielded favorable results.

The commission rates generally lean towards the lower end of the spectrum, necessitating a substantial influx of traffic to yield any semblance of revenue.

The products you are endorsing are available on Amazon, which boasts a formidable website and holds one of the highest domain scores globally due to its status as one of the most highly visited online platforms. Consequently, their product pages will consistently dominate your search rankings, implying that unless you possess alternative sources of web traffic beyond search engine optimization (SEO), your merchandise will not be discoverable through product reviews.

One further rationale for my disapproval of endorsing Amazon products stems from the fact that their tracking cookie has a mere 24-hour duration. The website experiences such a high volume of traffic that if an individual returns to the site within 48 hours after initially clicking on your link, it is presumed that they arrived via an alternative source. Furthermore, the lack of dependence on external assistance to generate website traffic and promote their products implies that they do not prioritize competitive rates and extended cookie durations. They do not rely on your presence for their sustenance.

Companies that prioritize the success and growth of their affiliates demonstrate greater generosity in their offerings and express deep gratitude for their affiliates. This is not Amazon.

There exist alternative approaches through which you may integrate their products into your articles, aside from straightforward product reviews. Therefore, if you desire to do so, consider focusing on crafting articles centered around comparing various products. "X Product vs. "Y Product", or "Ranking of the Top X Products on Amazon".

The comparison article for the mom blog that we operate currently holds the third position, listed below two Amazon search results. When conducting a search for double strollers priced below $200, it is noteworthy that mommybear.org ranks third among the results on Google. These categories of articles have the potential to achieve high rankings; however, it is apparent from the aforementioned outcome that our primary objective remains focused on surpassing Amazon.

If your aim is to reach a broad audience through social media platforms and produce popular product videos, incorporating Amazon affiliate marketing could be a valuable addition to your business strategy. If your objective is to generate search traffic through your marketing strategy, it would be advisable to refrain from pursuing this option. Amazon is too strong.

An effective tactic that I have observed yielding remarkable results is the utilization of concise video content. Individuals will create a Facebook Reel wherein they exhibit a compilation of "Top X Amazon Finds to Assist You in YZ", subsequently linking to all the featured products within the initial comment. These videos garnered substantial viewership, owing to the allure they held for individuals seeking to discover and explore novel and advantageous products that were previously unfamiliar to them. Ensure prompt and thorough elucidation of how the products effectively address a specific issue, and consistently disclose your affiliation when providing hyperlinks.

You are required to upload your video on Facebook Reels, as it is the sole platform that affords the option to include hyperlinks within the comment section. I have not personally experimented with this approach as I harbor some disillusionment towards Amazon. Nonetheless, I may consider undertaking it at some point in the proximate future to evaluate its effectiveness. It is an effective method for generating the substantial amount of traffic required for Amazon's success.

In my view, there exist a multitude of superior programs available for promotion. Therefore, while you may choose to consider Amazon, I tend to allocate my efforts elsewhere, as I prefer to pursue free search traffic.

SEO Research

General posts:

There is a complimentary extension available for chromium browsers known as the "SeoStack Keyword Tool." Proceed with the installation, access the application, and input the name of your product, navigating through inquiries and prepositions.

Please ensure that the CSV file is saved and consult this tutorial for instructions on how to perform the necessary data cleansing steps to render it compatible for utilization in the keyword planner.

Subsequently, employ the keyword planner to ascertain keywords that have reduced levels of competition (either low or medium) and increased levels of search volume (either high or medium).

Please record these keywords within a document and incorporate them within your posts as needed. This will assist you in achieving favorable on-page SEO results.

Niche Based Posts:

Take an additional stride, providing further precision.

Please reiterate the procedure in which we employed the Amazon search bar. However, this time, instead of employing letters, utilize your designated keyword and incorporate additional words such as "for," "to," "with," and so forth.

Please compile a list of outcomes following the previous procedure, and utilize SeoStack to search for the keywords, phrases, and sentences extracted from Amazon. Subsequently, proceed to export the CSV file, perform the necessary data cleansing, and subsequently proceed with the upload to the keyword planner.

Select the optimal key terms exhibiting reduced competition (low or moderate) and increased search volume (high or moderate). Store them in a designated file for later use in your posts that cater to specific niche topics.

Now that we have completed the SEO research, let us explore the process of crafting our posts.

Four categories of content that yield favorable results in conjunction with Amazon Affiliate Marketing.

General recommendation: adopt an amicable demeanor in your writing, convey authenticity, refrain from displaying any dubious or questionable intentions, and compose your text as if you were engaging in conversation with close acquaintances or relatives. Do not hesitate to employ humor, as individuals tend to gravitate towards those who are capable of eliciting laughter.

Writing a review

Users typically seek out reviews of a product in order to acquire comprehensive information regarding it. This encompasses a comprehensive portrayal as well as your personal assessment of the merchandise.

Typically, it can be challenging to provide an assessment on a product that you have not personally experienced. However, through extensive research, one can acquire sufficient knowledge to form an informed perspective.

Commence the investigation by verifying the information provided in official sources. Familiarize yourself with the product's description provided by the seller, as well as the visual aids such as pictures and videos that they have made available.

Subsequently, verify the information provided by the user. Peruse the customer feedback available on Amazon to ascertain the features that are particularly well-received by users. What are people hating?

Observe the visuals and visual recordings that have been posted, as they possess a genuine character devoid of any involvement from a marketing team. Engage in active video viewing on the YouTube platform to observe product demonstrations and explore comments section for valuable insights and feedback from users.

As evident from the present observation, the greater the number of reviews a product possesses, the more effortless it becomes to articulate one's thoughts about it. Therefore, kindly consider this aspect while deliberating upon the selection of a seller. In the upcoming chapter, we will discuss the process of obtaining links, as well as the criteria for selecting sellers and products.

Given the wealth of information available, endeavor to compose the posts with utmost candor.

The List

Lists are highly advantageous as they allow for efficient and expedient composition. In addition, we, as users, have a positive disposition toward them.

To compile a list, identify a common characteristic shared by five promotional products. Consider attributes such as color, user-friendliness, gender specificity, superiority, popularity, positive reviews, or distinctiveness.

Subsequently, it will be necessary to compose a concise narrative elucidating the shared attributes of said products.

Ultimately, compose a brief overview for any single item in question. You may incorporate additional details that enhance or detract from the viability of the product as an alternative. This would be more effective when applied to catalogs of potential substitutes for a given product.

Product A vs. Product B

Such posts prove to be beneficial for products that face competition from multiple brands. Some potential options for smartphones include Apple, Samsung, and even Xiaomi. Potential options for electric vehicles include brands such as Tesla, Chevrolet, or Mercedes-Benz. Regarding culinary utensils, notable options encompass Tefal, Le Creuset, and OXO.

In order to compose a comparative article, it will be necessary for you to select a specific item (such as an oven) and proceed to examine and contrast analogous models from two distinct brands.

Commence by analyzing the inherent characteristics, such as the composition of the material, the desirable attributes, and the functionalities offered by the programs, among others.

Subsequently, proceed to articulate your thoughts on the distinct qualities that render each of them exceptional. What deficiencies are evident in each of them, which contribute to their inferiority.

Additionally, it would be advisable to conduct a comparative analysis of the prices. This can be accomplished by compiling the information into a tabular format, either alongside the physical characteristics or appended at the conclusion of each product description.

How-to Guide

Such types of posts prove to be highly beneficial and effortless to compose.

• If you happen to retail white adhesive, it would be advisable to compose a piece detailing its application in crafting endeavors.

If you are engaged in the sale of fitness equipment, you have the opportunity to provide valuable content focused on instructions for its utilization or workout routines that incorporate its usage.

• If one is engaged in the sale of oven cleaner, it would be prudent to compose a piece detailing the proper method of oven cleaning that employs the use of the aforementioned product.

Bonus: Product use

The creation of such posts is rendered more challenging due to the requisite steps involved, which encompass the procurement of the product, its utilization, and the composition of an accompanying review.

You have the capability to produce a video as well.

Nevertheless, the customer highly values these kinds of posts. Make an effort to create one occasionally.

I advise against pursuing this strategy initially, as you will face challenges in establishing a prominent online presence within search engine rankings.

Furthermore, there exists a multitude of tasks on your website that hold considerable importance and must be addressed promptly.

Final advices

• Do not allow yourself to be immobilized by the pursuit of perfection. You are expected to compose a well-crafted post, but it does not necessarily have to be flawless. Please bear in mind that you have the option to revisit it at any time and make necessary adjustments.

• Carry out an extensive examination of the posts and engage in critical analysis, while refraining from feeling intimidated or disturbed by their content.

Competition serves as the paramount repository of insights and knowledge pertaining to your business. Engage in extensive reading and knowledge acquisition, subsequently implementing the acquired knowledge to enhance the functioning of your business, should you deem it beneficial.

• You possess adequate capabilities; refrain from undermining yourself by entertaining the notion that you lack competence.

• Exercise caution when engaging in self-sabotaging behaviors.

• Do not be apprehensive about the possibility of failure, and refrain from attempting to forecast the future as it exceeds the capacity of human beings. Commence your endeavors, exert utmost effort, and await the discernment of the world to determine the adequacy of your product or the necessity for its enhancement.

Guide to Developing a Website

Introduction

The hosting

One of the initial challenges I encountered at the outset was determining the most suitable hosting platform to employ. The web hosting I utilized as per the sequential lessons was extremely affordable, yet it fell short in terms of quality. Initially, when I encountered an issue, the Customer Service department failed to provide any assistance for a prolonged period of several weeks.

My experience with the second one, which I utilized for a personal blog, proved to be significantly superior. I encountered a technical concern regarding the SSL certificate, to which they responded promptly and provided assistance by furnishing a comprehensible article on the subject.

I would recommend initiating an exploration of highly regarded options with the most prestigious and well-regarded establishments in your country. Seek input from acquaintances and engage in discussions within relevant communities, exercising caution when considering reviews from individuals with potential affiliations, as their perspectives may not always align with genuine intentions. You may consider utilizing platforms such as TrustPilot.com to gauge user sentiment and gather insight on the options that align with your preferences.

Amazon Requisites

I additionally encountered difficulties in comprehending the expectations of Amazon. As an esteemed corporation, Amazon will undoubtedly prioritize safeguarding their brand reputation. They are disinclined to partake in fraudulent schemes, dubious enterprises, or the dissemination of unsolicited promotional content.

The sole piece of information I discovered indicates that it is necessary for me to include a statement within the posts emphasizing that "certain links may be affiliated, and as a result, I may receive a commission." This was acceptable to me and appeared legitimate, however, they did not provide further explication.

Therefore, I had to conduct a thorough examination of the Amazon Affiliate Policies, and I highly recommend that you review them as well. The information provided in these policies is comprehensive and unambiguous regarding their expectations from you.

Be independent

To establish any venture, one must undertake extensive learning and conducting thorough research. You will need to develop self-reliance as a learner, and in doing so, Google will become an invaluable resource.

We are fortunate to possess an abundance of freely accessible information on the internet. We additionally offer convenient communication channels through which individuals who have previously visited our establishment and are willing to provide assistance can be reached.

In the realm of programming, this phenomenon is widely prevalent, to the extent that the utilization of Google within professional settings encounters no hindrances or objections.

You should seek out individuals who are facing similar circumstances as yourself. These resources can be located within specialized forums and discords. Additionally, please ensure to examine the groups on WhatsApp, Telegram, and Facebook. In addition, Amazon has enabled the Discussion Boards associated with Amazon Associates.

Acquiring Lucrative Returns Through Ppc In Your Business

PPC, also known as Pay-Per-Click, is classified as one of the four foundational categories of search engines. PPC is also considered as one of the most viable approaches to targeted internet marketing. According to Forbes magazine, Pay Per Click (PPC) generates a staggering revenue of 2 billion dollars annually, and it is projected to steadily rise to approximately 8 billion dollars by the year 2008.

Please grant us the opportunity to examine the functioning of PPC Web directories.

These motors make postings and rate them in light of a bid sum the site proprietor will pay for each click from that web search tool. Sponsors engage in competitive bidding in order to secure top placements for a specific keyword or phrase.

The individual who places the highest bid on a particular keyword or phrase will subsequently have their website ranked as the top result in the Pay-Per-Click (PPC) search engines, followed by the second and third highest bidders, until all bidders for the same keyword or phrase have been accounted for. Your advertisements will be prominently displayed on the results pages based on the agreed-upon cost per click bid.

What strategies would you employ to generate revenue through the utilization of PPC in your affiliate marketing business?

Many affiliate programs typically offer compensation based on successful transactions or leads generated from visitors who have clicked through your website. The potential earnings derived from your income are typically contingent upon factors such as the quality of the site content and the demand in the market.

The motivation behind why you ought to integrate PPC into your subsidiary showcasing program is that profit are more straightforward to make than in some other sort of member program not utilizing PPC. In light of this, you will generate profits derived from the clickthroughs generated by your visitors on the sponsor's website. In contrast to particular endeavors, compensation is not based on individual transactions or actions.

PPC can be extremely creative of your site. By incorporating PPC web directories into your business

Within the membership program, you will indeed seek to derive advantages from those guests who may not be initially captivated by your offerings. Individuals with comparable behavior who depart from your website without subsequently revisiting.

You will not only receive commissions from individuals conducting online searches and finding the products and services they desire, but you will also have the opportunity to enhance the recognition of your website as a valuable resource. The guests who have found what they required from you site are probably going to return and audit what you are offering all the more intently. Subsequently, they will proceed to search the internet for alternative products.

This particular affiliate program also serves as a convenient means for you to generate supplemental revenue. For example, if a visitor to your website utilizes the PPC Web search tool to conduct a search and subsequently clicks on the anticipated advertisements, the advertisers' accounts will experience a deduction in response to that particular click. With

In return for this, you will be reimbursed a percentage ranging from 30% to 80% of the sum offered by the publicists.

PPC does not solely serve as a source of generating straightforward profits; rather, it can also facilitate the promotion and enhancement of your own website. A significant portion of the projects allow the commissions to be immediately allocated towards advertising, without any minimum earnings requirement. This is considered to be an effective approach to exchanging your prospective customers for individuals who are more inclined to make purchases of your products and services.

What are the potential outcomes if you integrate PPC into your affiliate program?

Pay-per-click (PPC) platforms commonly offer readily available affiliate tools that can be seamlessly integrated into your website. The search boxes, standards, text connections, and a limited number of 404-error pages stand out as the most universally acknowledged devices. The majority of web crawlers utilize bespoke configurations and are able to provide you with a private-label affiliate program. With the help of a few lines of code, you can seamlessly integrate a externally-hosted co-branded search engine onto your website, thereby enhancing its functionality.

The key advantages? An increase in monetary output, coupled with supplementary funds as an ancillary outcome. In addition to receiving lifetime commissions, when you have referred individuals who are website administrators to the motor.

Consider it. Where can one obtain such a wide array of benefits even before generating any revenue for their website? Understanding a selection of the most advantageous tools at your disposal for your partnership program is a valuable endeavor that should not be disregarded. They can be considered as a means of obtaining within a process of obtaining.

It would be wise to investigate the potential of integrating PPC web search tools into your affiliate program, as you would not want to miss out on the exceptional opportunity to enhance your profitability.

Leveraging Recommended Products to Enhance Net Profitability

In the realm of affiliate marketing, there exist various strategies through which one can enhance their earnings and sustain the progress they have diligently strived for thus far. The majority of the methods and strategies can be considerably enhanced without encountering any difficulties. Please refrain from proceeding to any location and refrain from seeking any form of encouragement. They can be accessed online, continuously throughout the day and every day of the week.

One of the more notable strategies for enhancing the core objective and sales of affiliate marketing is through the implementation of product recommendations. Many advertisers acknowledge that this method could potentially be one of the most effective means of promoting a specific product.

If the clients or visitors repose trust in you, they will also place trust in your recommendations. Nevertheless, exercise utmost care when employing this approach. Should you choose to solely promote ideas, your credibility will become greatly diminished. This phenomenon is particularly evident when suggestions are seemingly distorted and lacking substantial validity.

You are welcome to express any aspects or features of a particular product or service that you could readily forgo. Rather than detracting from your focal points, this will enhance the coherence of your proposal and generally enhance your credibility.

Furthermore, should your guests possess genuine interest in the product you are offering, they will eagerly welcome knowledge concerning its merits, drawbacks, and the ways in which it will benefit them.

When recommending a specific product, there are several notable aspects to consider in order to ensure its effective implementation and optimal advantages.

Exhibit expertise and authority as a proficient leader in your domain.

Please bear in mind the following basic principle: The decrease in cost disparity is directly proportional to the level of trust. If your guests perceive and acknowledge your expertise in your field, they are more inclined to make the purchase. On the contrary, if you do not exude a sense of assurance and belief in endorsing your products, customers are likely to harbor the same doubts and will likely seek out an alternative product or service that appears more trustworthy.

How would you present or arrange this aura of expertise? Through the provision of captivating and innovative arrangements, they would be deterred from seeking alternative options elsewhere. Please provide evidence to substantiate the functionality of your claimed assertions. Display prominent accolades and endorsements from esteemed and renowned individuals within relevant domains, naturally.

Refrain from engaging with publicity under any circumstances. It is more advisable to maintain a composed and assured demeanor, rather than raising one's voice and seeking attention. Furthermore, it is highly improbable that you would wish to come across as inexperienced and allow such conjecture to impact your prospective customers and clients, wouldn't you agree? It is advisable to present oneself as both composed and self-assured.

Additionally, it is important to note that possibilities should not be underestimated. They are actively seeking out experts and are likely to possess the same knowledge as you do. Given that you substantiate your claims with concrete facts and evidence, individuals would be willing to invest substantial sums of money, ranging from hundreds to even thousands, in support of your innovations. In any event, should you fail to do so, they possess the sophistication to actively examine and assess your competitors' offerings.

When making a recommendation, it is advisable to offer time-limited incentives. Individuals are currently familiar with the concept of offering gifts to promote their own products." "Individuals are presently acquainted with the notion of presenting gifts to endorse their own merchandise." "People are currently well-versed in the practice of gifting to promote their own goods. Nevertheless, a minority of individuals engage in this practice to promote affiliate products. Make an effort to present gifts that can enhance or acquire knowledge about your products or services.

Prior to providing suggestions for your item, it is expected that you should first conduct thorough testing and evaluation of the product. Endeavor to avoid the promotion of inferior products and services. Consider the length of time it took for you to establish credibility and trustworthiness with your audience. Merely a single significant mistake on your end is all it would take to eradicate it.

If possible, present recommendations of products in which you possess complete confidence. Prior to commencing, it is imperative to evaluate the support of the item to ensure that those to whom you intend to recommend it will not be left vulnerable in the event of an unforeseen issue.

Examine your affiliate market and evaluate the strategies you are implementing. It is possible that you are not adequately focusing on the recommendations concerning the necessary qualities of your items. Your strategy is not solely responsible for the success of your program.

Propose relevant items and join the ranks of distinguished individuals who have exemplified its value.

Chapter 4: Selecting a Specialized Field

Welcome to part two. In the following section, we shall delve into the importance of carefully choosing the appropriate niche for your blog. Selecting the appropriate field is essential for your success, as failure to do so may severely impede your future prospects. If, by any chance, you happen to choose an inappropriate niche for your blog, then you will have to bid farewell to your aspirations of becoming a professional blogger.

When it comes to selecting an appropriate niche for your blog, there are various factors to consider prior to finalizing the suitable topic. It is important to ensure that the topic you select for composition is not overly saturated, thereby indicating a scarcity of bloggers who have already written about it.

Surprisingly, there is no requirement for a highly specialized theme, indicating potential difficulties in directing individuals to the website. In summary, it would be advisable to ensure the presence of excellent affiliate options for the niche. While it is true that a majority of specialties have alternative options available, one cannot overlook the question of whether these alternatives will yield a beneficial outcome.

In this segment, our aim is to present to you the most sought-after methodologies for identifying a niche that is tailored to your individual skills and expertise. Furthermore, I will provide you with several techniques to identify a topic to write about that is currently attracting an optimal level of web traffic, facilitating your opportunity to generate income. Immediately, let us now delve into the foundational aspects of this component.

Select a specialized field that you hold in high regard

If you are not approaching your writing with a serious mindset, it is unlikely that you will earn any profit from it.

Individuals possess an exceptional ability to detect individuals who lack connection or relevance to the topic at hand. It is paramount that the niche you select as the foundation for your blog holds considerable personal appeal to you, or at the very least, evokes some degree of genuine interest.

The optimal method to discover your niche is to ponder upon your personal passions and recreational pursuits. In the event that I have a strong inclination towards yoga and engage in regular yoga practice, it may present itself as an option for you. Reflect on your personal pursuits or areas of interest. Each individual possesses a particular interest or pastime that brings them joy. I have a strong conviction that you also possess it, therefore uncover and compose it.

Micro-level specialization

Once you have chosen a topic to write about, it is imperative to acquaint yourself with the competition. To ascertain this information, conduct a thorough examination of your area of expertise using the Google search engine, specifically focusing on locating the "About" section located directly beneath the search bar.

You will observe a numerical figure that is likely to be in the range of millions. In order to identify the appropriate specialization, it is advisable to consider a figure below 50 million or exceeding 1 million, as this range can be deemed as the optimal criteria. Any amount exceeding 50 million would result in a significant level of involvement, whereas a sum below 1 million would indicate a diminished likelihood of achieving profitability.

Affiliate marketing

In subsequent sections, we will delve deeper into partner advertising. It is crucial that you conduct thorough research and ascertain the opportunities within your chosen field prior to commencing your blog. For readers unfamiliar with the concept of affiliate marketing, it pertains to the practice of featuring a product on your blog with a link that is exclusively relevant to your website. Whenever an individual opts to make a purchase of that specific product through your link, you will be eligible to receive a commission.

Affiliate marketing is the primary source of income for the majority, if not all, bloggers, thus it is crucial not to disregard this progression. To determine if your topic is suitable for an affiliate program, it is recommended to visit Amazon.com and thoroughly examine all the products associated with your chosen niche that are available for purchase. If they have a substantial inventory of products available for you to promote, then you have found the suitable option. In a subsequent section, we will delve into additional alternatives pertaining to partner promotion. However, for the present moment, place emphasis on Amazon and the range of products they offer.

Monetizing

By opting to monetize your blog site, you will grant permission for Google to display advertisements on your blog. Whenever individuals engage with that advertisement, you will undoubtedly generate revenue. The most effective approach to ascertain the level of Google advertising in your specific niche is to perform a search using your specific "keyword."

If the topic of interest pertains to yoga exercise, utilize the search bar on Google and input 'yoga exercise' as your search query. The higher the frequency of advertisements within your specific niche that you encounter, the greater your potential for earning revenue through the monetization of your blog. Monetizing your blog can be a highly effective strategy for generating additional income, particularly if your blog receives significant traffic.

Final research

Presently, in order to ensure the acquisition of the handle pertaining to your chosen subject, it is necessary to access the platform known as "Google Trends". This is where you will ascertain the frequency with which your subject is being searched and the level of interest among individuals who actively seek articles within your specific niche. Simply input your search query into the search engine, and it will present you with a graphical representation.

Please ensure that you are taking into account a chart containing a minimum of 5 years' worth of data. Presently, if your portrayal persists at a consistently high level without any fluctuations, then you have indeed made a wise choice of the subject matter. In the event that your chart exhibits a progressive decline over the years, it is then appropriate for you to explore a fresh blog topic.

After thoroughly reviewing all of these criteria, you will have identified the suitable niche and can promptly commence your blog. If that is not the case, I kindly request that you reconsider your topics and come up with a new one that does fulfill all of the aforementioned criteria.

However, it is imperative to ensure that you are deriving monetary benefits from your blog rather than merely writing for it. Continuously engage in browsing and persevere in exploration, and eventually you will discover your treasured subject. Rest assured, it is imperative that you possess the capability to identify your subject amidst various frames.

Drawbacks Of Affiliate Marketing

There exist several drawbacks associated with affiliate marketing that it is important for you to be cognizant of prior to embarking on this venture.

To begin with, it can prove to be challenging to generate a substantial amount of traffic towards your affiliate links. A comprehensive knowledge of search engine optimization and effective strategies for attracting visitors to your website is imperative.

Additionally, it is imperative to possess a substantial amount of financial savings in order to withstand a prolonged period without generating any substantial profits from your endeavors. Affiliate marketing is far from being a shortcut to wealth or rapid financial success.

Furthermore, establishing connections with fellow bloggers and marketers may pose challenges for novices in the field. Establishing meaningful relationships with individuals who have the potential to facilitate the promotion of your products and services requires a considerable investment of time and effort.

However, notwithstanding these drawbacks, affiliate marketing remains a highly lucrative avenue for generating income on the internet.

If you demonstrate a commitment to exerting effort, you will undeniably witness positive outcomes in the realm of Affiliate Marketing.

Are you intrigued by the concept of affiliate marketing? That is excellent news, as it presents a lucrative opportunity to generate income through online means. However, there are several obstacles that must be overcome in order to achieve success.

The primary obstacle lies in identifying a high-quality product for promotional purposes. It is imperative to identify content that holds relevance to your target audience and aligns with your personal convictions. If one endorses a product in which they lack conviction, it will become evident to their audience, ultimately resulting in a loss of trust.

The next obstacle involves the establishment of high-caliber content.

This is crucial if you desire to capture the attention of your target audience and successfully convert them into paying customers. You are required to generate content that is captivating, enlightening, and compelling.

One further obstacle entails the establishment of a roster of individuals who have opted to receive updates. This is crucial when striving to generate income through affiliate marketing. It is imperative to cultivate a compilation of individuals who possess a genuine interest in your discourse, ensuring that they receive timely updates regarding your most recent offerings and promotions.

If one is able to surmount these obstacles, affiliate marketing can prove to be a lucrative avenue for generating online income.

Chapter 11: Essential Insights Regarding the Distinctions Between Google Adsense and Affiliate Marketing

◉ Gaining access to an Affiliate network is considerably simpler compared to obtaining approval for Google AdSense.

◉ Affiliate Marketing offers a more substantial commission compared to other Cost Per Click (CPC) platforms such as Google AdSense, Yahoo, and Chitika.

◉ A majority of the affiliate companies provide PayPal as a payment option, while Google AdSense and Yahoo do not. However, they now offer NEFT - National Electronic Fund Transfer.

◉ A wide array of affiliate products can be discovered for nearly every niche topic; however, it is important to note that placing AdSense advertisements within a specific niche is not permissible.

⦿ Google AdSense or Yahoo provides ongoing income, whereas Affiliate marketing provides a lump sum payment.

⦿ Google has exclusive control over the management of AdSense, while numerous affiliate companies, both small and large, can be found on the internet, such as JVzoo, Clickbank, CJ, Amazon, and others.

⦿ Affiliate advertisements offer greater appeal and control, while we possess limited control over the AdSense cost-per-click model.

Based on the aforementioned points and numerous factual data, it can be concluded that the Affiliate marketing program is a more financially rewarding and advantageous option compared to any CPC-based model operated by entities such as Google or Yahoo. However, it is important to note that before arriving at a final judgment, there are some additional aspects that should be considered:

Affiliate marketing products or links are effective exclusively on specific pages, while any page of your blog or website that fails to generate revenue for you does not fulfill this purpose.

On the contrary, AdSense provides a viable solution for pages that are incompatible with affiliate marketing products.

Hence, it can be inferred that Google AdSense acts as the fundamental cornerstone for bloggers and webmasters to generate income online, as it enables monetary rewards.

In contrast, within the context of an affiliate sale, we have the opportunity to earn a commission ranging from 1 to

100 dollars, contingent on the specific product you are promoting.

Therefore, I would recommend considering a combination of both Google Adsense and Affiliate sales as viable options for you.

Chapter 12: Is it possible to place both Amazon Affiliate and Adsense on the same page?

Allow me to cite the Amazon Affiliate Ads as an illustrative instance, given their status as a widely recognized and well-established affiliate program within the online realm.

You have the option to substitute it with any alternative platform or website such as eBay, hosting affiliate programs, or other affiliate programs that come to mind.

Indeed, it is permissible to position Affiliate advertisements alongside AdSense advertisements on the same webpage, without transgressing any AdSense policies.

Presented here is an authoritative AdSense support page wherein it is explicitly stated: "Affiliate or limited-text links are indeed permitted."

Prior to engaging in the placement of affiliate banner ads and link ads on your blog or website, it is imperative to be aware of several crucial considerations.

If the quantity of advertisements or affiliate banners/links exceeds that of the original content, it poses a risk to the security of your Google AdSense account.

Thus, endeavor to restrict the quantity of advertisements displayed on your blog, while prioritizing the incorporation of valuable and high-quality content within your website or blog.

⦿ It is imperative that your affiliate advertisements refrain from directing users to content that is in violation of the AdSense policies. Example: Content of a mature nature, including alcohol and drug-related themes.

Google AdSense considers any ads present on a webpage, whether from different ad networks or affiliate programs, to be integral to the overall content. Consequently, these ads are expected to adhere to the prescribed content guidelines established by Google.

⦿ Ensure that you employ No-follow attributes when incorporating Affiliate links on your blog or website. Although not directly related to AdSense, incorporating the Nofollow tag is considered a commendable approach from an SEO perspective.

Technological Advancements That Confer Benefits To Affiliates

Marketers

Once you have made the decision to pursue a career as an affiliate marketer, you will have access to a range of tools and software options that can greatly streamline your work. The technology landscape today encompasses an array of resources such as website development tools, email marketing platforms, and market research solutions, among others.

Website Tools

The creation of a website that can successfully convert visitors into customers necessitates thorough deliberation in the process of choosing a domain name, web hosting service, website development platform, and landing page automation tool. This will enable you to achieve greater efficiency and reduce both physical and mental burden. The subsequent tools will prove beneficial in completing all tasks.

Name of the Website

Acquiring a domain name is an initial and crucial step that must be undertaken to commence generating earnings through affiliate marketing. This will enable you to develop a website that is customized to the demographic most likely to be converted into clientele for your enterprise. Select a suitable title for your website that incorporates a pertinent keyword, doesn't exceed an optimal length, and remains easily memorable, culminating in a ".com" extension. When seeking an economical alternative to procure domain names, Namecheap.com proves to be an exceptional online platform.

Website Hosting

Once you have acquired the domain name for your website, the subsequent requirement will be website hosting. It is advisable to seek clarification from the host prior to purchasing your domain, as occasionally they may present an opportunity wherein the domain is gratuitously provided upon prepayment for hosting services. A reputable website host should possess a minimum uptime rate of 99 percent, deliver exceptional customer service, and offer a website interface that is user-friendly and intuitive. MomWebs.com is a highly recommended choice, particularly in instances where individuals are at the preliminary stages of website development and lack expertise in this field. They offer exceptional care and service to their clientele.

Website Builder

In addition, it is essential to undertake the establishment or arrangement of a well-crafted affiliate website of superior standards. Self-hosted WordPress is widely regarded as one of the most prevalent and efficient alternatives for this particular undertaking. For acquiring further information, one may consult WordPress.org. This website builder is user-friendly, affordable or potentially cost-free, and most significantly, it possesses excellent functionality and continues to be favored by search engines, thereby highlighting its effectiveness. This differs from WordPress.com, as it operates through the utilization of self-hosted WordPress.

Landing Page Builder

Once you have completed all other tasks, it would be advisable to utilize a landing page builder. You can achieve this objective at no cost by utilizing a self-hosted WordPress platform and simply generating a new webpage. However, it is important to note that the level of automation on this page will be considerably less compared to the other pages.

Implementing automation processes can effectively enhance your earning potential by reducing the need for manual task execution. Instapage.com presents a compelling choice for individuals in search of automated software specifically designed for creating landing pages. If you opt to promote your business utilizing a robust platform like Infusionsoft.com, it is already encompassed within your bundle. The utilization of this particular software will mechanize your sales funnels in such a manner that it will create the perception that your website has undergone a metamorphosis into an automated teller machine.

Email Marketing

You cannot circumvent the necessity of implementing email marketing strategies as it plays a pivotal role in the success of your business. It epitomizes one of the most efficacious and meritorious approaches to marketing, currently accessible in the contemporary era. The efficacy of email marketing surpasses social media marketing by a significant margin. This implies that you will be required to obtain leads and systematically transmit emails to your respective clientele. AWeber.com has emerged as a highly favored alternative, alongside the acclaimed platforms ConvertKit.com and ActiveCampaign.com. In conjunction with your landing page builder, these tools will substantially streamline the process.

Research on the Market

To ensure the effectiveness of your endeavors as an affiliate marketer, conducting extensive market research is imperative. Failure to conduct thorough research may result in the execution of futile actions, leading to a lack of progress. Rather than engaging in conjecture, it would be advisable to conduct the requisite investigation. One can conduct competitor analysis through the utilization of software tools like iSpionage.com, while exploration of popular subjects can be efficiently carried out by leveraging tools such as Google Trends.

The Production of Traffic

Establishing a prosperous affiliate marketing enterprise can also be achieved through significant investments in tools and resources that facilitate the generation of website traffic. In light of this, it is paramount to obtain a substantial volume of meticulously targeted website traffic if you wish to attain the desired results aligned with the goals and objectives set during the establishment phase.

The AdEspresso.com platform, developed by Hootsuite, offers a valuable application that streamlines the intricate tasks associated with managing and executing social media advertising campaigns on a substantial level. You will possess the opportunity to execute visually appealing and efficiently optimized advertisements across the foremost social media platforms.

Through the implementation of the Facebook pixel on your website and the utilization of Facebook Ads, you will gain the ability to execute retargeting and remarketing endeavors directly within the Facebook platform. Subsequently, you proceed to display a targeted advertisement exclusively visible to past customers, a strategy proven to effectively enhance both footfall and sales figures.

After being configured, the software on RecurPost.com will autonomously and unpredictably disseminate your blog entries across the social networking platforms you have selected.

Do not disregard the importance of sending an email as well. By making use of the automatic blog post sharing capabilities offered by your email marketing software, it is advisable to promptly notify your email recipients regarding the release of any newly published blog posts.

Monitoring and transforming information

The supplementary resources required to enhance your success as an affiliate marketer include tools that enable you to monitor the effectiveness of your endeavors and tools that facilitate the conversion of your audience. It is imperative that Google Analytics is implemented on every single website. It is entirely devoid of any charge, and it exhibits commendable performance. Ultimately, Google continues to reign as the preeminent choice among search engine platforms. This implies that you must adhere to their recommendations.

PrettyLinks.com is a highly commendable choice worthy of consideration when seeking a link monitoring service. You have the option to customize the software on your website, enabling the automatic inclusion of a link to your affiliate program whenever specific phrases are referenced. This approach represents an exceptional means of streamlining your recommendations and effectively monitoring click-through rates and conversions.

Marketing with Content

One method of enhancing the volume of traffic from your ideal target audience is through the dissemination of content that aligns with their interests. To produce captivating content, it is imperative to carry out thorough research, ensure its comprehensibility, and ascertain its overall appeal. Furthermore, it is imperative to ensure a consistent and systematic delivery of content. This constitutes an additional significant facet. With the aid of these tools, you ought to be capable of accomplishing it.

When embarking upon the task of conducting research, the most advisable course of action is to utilize the resources of Google Search and Google Website Tools as they provide the most sound and logical options. These locations should be your primary areas of focus. That is the juncture from which it would be fitting to commence. Nevertheless, there are remarkable software options that can be accessed for a fee, which, depending on the subject matter being examined, can be utilized with even greater efficacy. Some of the tools that may be of utility include conducting inquiries on social media platforms, conducting research on rival entities, and procuring an organization's goods or services to gain access to their internal data.

Revision: Prior to publication, be it a blog post or a product, it is imperative to ensure its comprehensibility for the intended audience through diligent editing. To achieve this objective, it is essential to ascertain the target audience and identify their preferred communication style. Furthermore, it is imperative that you possess advanced proficiency in the language or locate a proficient individual who can provide assistance. Furthermore, websites like Grammarly.com provide services for obtaining editing assistance. Nevertheless, the program presents a notable obstacle in that it has the potential to generate confusion for individuals who lack clarity regarding the necessary actions.

Visual elements — eventually, it will be necessary to create enticing visual components to enhance the aesthetic appeal and visual impact of your blog posts, social media updates, eBooks, and other creative undertakings. Canva.com is a viable choice for individuals lacking proficiency in graphic design; nonetheless, engaging the services of a proficient graphic designer also holds merit in executing this undertaking.

Regarding the aspects of marketing, scheduling, and preparing promotional activities for your affiliate company, there is a substantial amount of work involved. Scheduling - There is an extensive range of tasks that need to be addressed with regards to marketing. Nevertheless, CoSchedule.com could prove to be advantageous; it serves as a comprehensive marketing suite, integrating a marketing calendar, content organizer, social organizer, and various other functionalities into a single, convenient platform.

You may potentially necessitate the aid of an additional individual to strategize and produce the content for your affiliate enterprise. There is no need for you to undertake all of the responsibilities by yourself. You may consider hiring a professional content writer to offer their assistance, or alternatively, you could utilize content that is accompanied by private label rights to supplement and enhance your current content.

Utilizing valuable technology specifically designed for marketers is a crucial approach for affiliate marketers seeking advancement. It is essential to consistently review the fine print prior to acquiring or utilizing any novel technological devices, as certain devices explicitly prohibit actions like affiliate marketing and mandate the disclosure of such intentions. It is highly advisable to familiarize yourself with the guidelines, as this will furnish you with comprehensive instructions on the proper utilization of every product you acquire.

Factors To Consider When Selecting Your Target Market

Welcome to Stage 2 of this guide. I kindly request your utmost attention as you will be acquiring invaluable insights that will aid you in identifying a remarkably lucrative product.

What is your approach to identifying a market?

This particular demographic or market is further subdivided based on factors such as geographical location, ethnicity, income level, gender, age, and other relevant criteria.

Typically, the process of conducting market analysis and demographic assessment takes place during the initial conceptualization and design phase of a product. However, it is also possible to undertake demographic assessment when you are attempting to reintroduce the product to a new market and different demographic.

Why is it essential to carefully select your target market?

The identification of the target market dictates the suitable positioning of your product within the overall framework. Consider the scenario where you endeavor to introduce a novel vehicle that demonstrates economic features such as fuel efficiency, stylish design, comfort, and exceptional value for the price.

Now, let us consider your target market, consisting of individuals who possess a refined taste in automobiles, substantial wealth, and enjoy a prominent social standing and prestige. It is highly improbable that you will achieve any sales within this particular target market.

The rationale behind this statement is that this particular sector of the overall market exhibits a lack of interest in automobiles that offer efficiency and good value for money. They require vehicles that can enhance their social standing while aligning with their power and affluent lifestyle. They desire status symbols that can amplify their power and prestige, rather than prioritizing efficiency and cost-effectiveness.

The selection of an appropriate target market holds the potential to determine whether your product achieves resounding success or becomes a failure. Consider the case of the Tata Nano, widely acclaimed as the most inexpensive automobile on a global scale. Even amidst the initial reports regarding the progress of the automobile, the Tata family successfully sparked substantial anticipation surrounding this vehicle. It was marketed as the most economical automobile available, priced at approximately $2400 (at prevailing exchange rates).

What rendered it even more striking was the additional declaration of its safety credentials. Following the initial announcement, the launch prices experienced a substantial increase until the vehicle was finally released at a reasonably elevated cost. This car was _promised to change the average Indian drives and were primarily targeted at the two wheeler section of the Indian middle class._

Despite the initial sluggishness in sales and the initial setbacks encountered with the car, it appears that the general public has begun to embrace the vehicle and sales are now experiencing a notable upturn. If the Tata company had focused their attention on a more economically privileged segment of the population, it is likely that the car would have been abandoned and deemed a complete failure.

The importance of identifying and targeting your specific market segment is crucial if your intention is to enhance your revenue. In the aforementioned example, the commencement was executed accurately and its focus was strategically aimed at the appropriate audience in order to garner optimal engagement and intrigue.

In certain instances, an incisive marketing strategy is also indispensable in establishing a presence within the *market. Once again, taking the example of automobiles, let us consider the scenario where a globally recognized brand is venturing into an emerging market that entails a significant number of prospective car consumers.*

One potential approach would be to introduce a product that is the most promising option. In the case of India, the prosperous and extensive middle class emerges as a formidable and substantial segment. It essentially embodies the marketing strategy employed by major players in the midsize car market. This segment requires automobiles that possess contemporary design, exhibit high fuel efficiency, prioritize safety, and offer exceptional value in terms of cost. When embarking upon the introduction of a new vehicle within this particular market segment, it is of paramount importance to bear in mind the following considerations. The strategy employed by Hyundai Motor Corporation serves as a prime example. It commenced by introducing a line-up of compact vehicles in order to rival the acclaimed Maruti Suzuki brand.

Presently, Hyundai holds the esteemed position of being the second largest automobile manufacturer in India. It is noteworthy that Hyundai's two key production facilities in India also function as the primary exporters of automobiles in the country. After successfully captivating the emotions and intellect of the compact vehicle market, they have proceeded to introduce their high-end automobiles with a focus on the affluent consumer segment of the market.

What are the strategies employed to target the market?

"The Marketing strategies can be categorized as follows:

Single segment strategy
The focus of this business strategy is directed towards a particular market segment, to which a specialized product mix is tailored and promoted. For small enterprises with restricted marketing, distribution, and production resources, this methodology remains the preferred approach as it effectively serves the

portion of the market that aligns with their current scale and capacity.

Frequently, large corporations that employ a targeted marketing approach may opt to explore product acceptance and the viability of a broader marketing strategy through means such as a limited pilot launch in select markets.

Selective specialization

This approach revolves around the strategic marketing of various products towards distinct market segments, thereby cultivating a diversified product mix. Occasionally, a product may be promoted with a modification in marketing strategy and branding in order to establish differentiation and cater to the desired market segment.

Product specialization

Companies frequently exhibit a propensity to focus exclusively on a singular product, subsequently promoting it across various market segments. Their approach is characterized by a significant *degree of product specialization, accompanied by a concentrated focus on a singular product.*

Market specialization

When a company focuses on a particular segment of the market and subsequently employs distinct product assortments and strategies to promote them, it represents an instance of market specialization. For instance, in the amidst of the automotive industry, if a company exclusively focuses on the production of trucks and targets the particular segment of consumers with an interest in trucks, this exemplifies an illustration of market specialization.

To Conduct An Investigation Into The Financial Viability Of A Market

Conducting market research is essential in the realm of online marketing, as well as any other marketing strategy, to assess the profitability of the product to be marketed. The assessment of profitability encompasses, though is not restricted to, evaluating the product's market demand, examining its level of competition, and determining the feasibility of introducing additional suppliers in light of the existing demand and supply conditions.

The significance of conducting profitability research

In straightforward economic terms, when the quantity supplied exceeds the quantity demanded, it can lead to a scenario wherein a price war may ensue. The most favorable course of action would entail entering a market characterized by an insufficiency of supply in relation to demand, coupled with the presence of a robust inflationary environment and ample opportunities for financial gain.

The assessment of profitability also serves to guarantee the attainment of satisfactory profits by marketing the aforementioned product, thereby enabling the realization of your revenue objectives.

Engaging in transactions within a market characterized by minimal profitability, insufficient to warrant the exertion of efforts towards sourcing, stocking, marketing, selling, and providing customer support and after-sales service, constitutes a grave error. It is imperative to conduct a thorough profitability assessment prior to the introduction of the product.

What is the appropriate method for conducting a profitability analysis?

When conducting an investigation into online profitability, it is recommended to assess the market in which you plan to promote and sell your products. Suppose you intend to offer an electronic book for sale on eBay, covering the topic of "canine house training."

Your initial step should involve examining eBay personally in order to ascertain the level of competition from other sellers offering comparable dog training books. As outlined in the introductory paragraph, the lower the supply in relation to the demand, the greater the potential for profitability.

One can establish a higher price point and generate greater financial gains compared to operating with a narrow profit margin. There are multiple instruments available to ascertain the relative abundance of products associated with the same or corresponding keyword. Suppose you desire to ascertain the quantity of products listed on eBay using the keyword phrase 'dog training'.

There exists a research tool known as Terapeak that can offer significant insights into the overall quantity of these listings, the rate at which they are sold, and the average price at which these products are sold.

Cool!

Isn't it?

This information is of great importance when conducting product profitability analysis, as well as determining relevant market dynamics and assessing product demand within that specific market. Based on the findings provided in this research material, it is possible to reconsider the pricing strategy and assess the feasibility of selling the product to the intended target market.

Checking the demand.

The subsequent step to undertake involves determining the market demand for books pertaining to dog training on the e-commerce platform eBay. Once again, an increased level of demand will be advantageous for both you and the likelihood of achieving profitability.

An alternative way to express the same information in a formal tone could be: "To ascertain the level of demand for a particular item on eBay, it is advisable to assess the relative selling rate, which can be determined by referring to the information obtained through the utilization of Terapeak, as mentioned in the preceding paragraph." This should provide you with an understanding of the rapid pace at which the competitive products on this site are moving.

Checking the competition.
The greater the number of competitors in the target market, the more intense the competition and challenges will be in terms of selling your product. It is recommended to examine the pricing strategies of your competitors, as well as their comparative sales performance and selling tactics, prior to establishing your own price.
If they are selling at an elevated price point and not garnering sufficient sales, this should provide you with an indication of the market's response.

Certain markets exhibit a significant degree of price sensitivity. Subtle variations will ultimately dictate the distinction between successful sales and no transactions occurring.

If your product is aimed at providing home improvement tips, a topic that has already been extensively covered, and you are targeting a price-sensitive segment, it is likely that a higher price will deter potential buyers, while your competitors, who offer a lower price point, will successfully sell their products.

Competitive intelligence.

Examine your foremost competitor and acquire comprehensive information regarding their selling tactics and product offering. Please examine your product and your pricing strategy. If there exists a potential that your products possess distinctive advantages over your competitors, it is evidently more advantageous to emphasize those areas in your marketing strategy and employ them as your unique selling proposition (USP).

Product trend.
Monitoring market trends and aligning with customer preferences are integral factors in ensuring profitability assessment. This aids not only your present product sales but also your future sales, as the inability to forecast or evaluate customer trends and demands may cause you to overlook valuable insights or strategies that your more market-savvy competitors may not miss.

Product sourcing.
An essential aspect in assessing the profitability of a product is to identify a stable and reliable source for its procurement. Let's suppose you are engaged in the trade of internationally sourced White coffee from Ipoh, which happens to be a city in Malaysia, and marketing it through online platforms.
Your initial focus should be on securing a reliable supplier of the product from

Ipoh, ensuring that you have more than one supplier option available. This way, you can anticipate the re-order level of your current stock and have a dependable source to obtain fresh inventory.

If the reliability of your product sourcing is not assured, it not only poses a potential profitability issue due to order cancellations, but also endangers your reputation with your customers. Ensuring dependability also entails maintaining a stable price, with no risk of the supplier intentionally withholding supply or seeking excessive profits at your expense.

Additional expenses associated with the sale of the product.

Other factors that should be taken into account during an analysis of a product's profitability are the costs associated with the handling, storage, transportation, and distribution involved in the sale of the product. These expenses serve as significant factors in the sales process and have a direct impact on both the final pricing and the overall profitability margin.

Chapter 5

E

Highly efficient and innovative techniques and equipment

Due to the amalgamation of generating substantial sales through the establishment of a dedicated audience and the magnitude associated with the act of selling a multitude of tangible products, encompassing digital, services, and physical goods, the efficacy of this approach is considerably enhanced.

In addition, it is essential to consider that due to the diverse range of affiliate products available on your website, you possess the capability to sell products that are commonly regarded as speculative or ambitious sales opportunities. An example? I had previously facilitated a sale by leveraging an affiliate link for marketing purposes, aimed at promoting and selling an MBA program. This transaction was conducted via the renowned affiliate platform, EDx, known for its significant revenue-generating capabilities.

The program serves as a prime illustration, albeit necessitating prior registration.

Whatisthedifficulty? Managing and balancing such a multitude of diverse tasks can be quite challenging. Hence, prominent and professional enterprises opt for technological solutions that streamline this endeavor and grant them the opportunity to tap into highly lucrative online affiliate networks.

The Indispensable Tools for Achieving Remarkable Success in Affiliate Marketing

Genius Link is one of the available tools that can be utilized. One has the option to link multiple accounts to Genius (https://www.geni.us/) and subsequently incorporate the respective affiliate programs within each of these accounts. This method is especially effective when used with Amazon, as it allows for the addition of accounts corresponding to each of the various regional versions of the platform. This significantly enhances the convenience of the Amazon shopping experience.

Upon clicking on any of the links, the user will be automatically redirected to the corresponding localized version of Amazon based on their geographical location. Thus, there is no concern of losing potential customers. Moreover, it is possible to install various software applications, such as iTunes, Barnes & Noble, and Best Buy, on your computer.

To promptly establish a connection to Amazon through this website, it is recommended to copy the URL of the sales page and subsequently insert it into the designated field after duplicating it. If you have the Chrome plugin installed, simply click the button conveniently located within your browser to effortlessly access the page.

Additionally, an alternative choice known as Trackonomics is accessible through the website: https://www.trackonomics.net. This tool operates in a similar fashion as the previous one; however, it provides you with the capability to incorporate products from an extensive selection of affiliates.

Such elements encompass the aforementioned EDx platform. Furthermore, Trackonomics provides the capability to conduct product searches across a diverse range of affiliate accounts, empowering you to choose the option that yields the highest level of monetary benefit.

If you are engaged in the sale of smartphones, you now have the opportunity to assess the potential commission on a particular smartphone by comparing the commission received from selling it through Amazon with the commission obtained through direct sales from the manufacturer. To phrase it differently, in the event that you are engaged in the sale of a smartphone, you are now able to assess and contrast the commission rate associated with said smartphone. In contrast to Best Buy and all other available alternatives.

With the utilization of either of these programs, you also have the capability to monitor and analyze clicks and purchases. This valuable feature enables you to ascertain the popularity of your links, identify any malfunctioning links, and assess your monetary earnings over a specific timeframe.

Theoneandonlydrawback? Trackonomicscomeswithawhoppingmonthly fee of $500. Nevertheless, an opportunity for a complimentary trial is available. During this interim period, Genius Link offers full functionality at no cost.

CHAPTER 5

More Instruments

These tools will enhance your ability to enhance your affiliate profits; however, there are numerous supplementary options accessible to individuals seeking to develop a more efficient business strategy and sales process.

As an illustration, if your objective is to monitor the performance of your website and its individual pages, it is advisable to employ Google Analytics.

This tool is highly recommended for accomplishing the task. You have the capability to monitor your rankings for various terms, optimize those terms, and subsequently analyze the effectiveness of different sites in driving traffic to the sales page while determining the most profitable routes.

Similarly, utilizing solutions that facilitate the implementation of A/B testing on your landing page can contribute to its optimization, resulting in a substantial increase in conversions.

Conclusion

Y

You have now been equipped with all the necessary information to establish a highly lucrative business centered around affiliate marketing. I strongly advise adhering to the suggestions provided in this literature and exploring the avenue of retailing tangible merchandise.

possess wide-ranging appeal and considerable pricing, along with the conventional offerings of digital eBooks and courses. It is within your discretion to decide between pursuing a simplistic approach or setting ambitious goals, however, I strongly advise that you adhere to the recommendations provided within the pages of this book.

Thetraditionalmethodforsellingaffiliatep roductsisquitestraightforward:

• Determine an appropriate digital offering and procure an affiliate hyperlink. • Develop a sales webpage. • Embed the hyperlink within the sales page. • Integrate the URL within the sales page. • Assimilate the link into the sales page. • Incorporate the web address within the sales page. • Increase the flow of visitors to the sales page through both your own website and various other marketing channels

• Exercise patience until the product's demand dwindles, and subsequently commence the process anew.

I highly recommend that you consider implementing some minor modifications to this model to enhance your profitability and establish a business strategy that is more viable in the long run.

The updated strategy is outlined below:

• Develop and maintain a professional website aimed at fostering a favorable perception of yourself and cultivating an audience that appreciates and values your work. o To accomplish this,

CONCLUSION

Produce content that is authentically innovative and manifests unwavering passion, complemented by a compelling visual representation and a definitive purpose statement.

• In the interim, endeavor to distribute a substantial quantity of compact digital commodities, physical products available on Amazon, and services by means of articles and websites that you endorse utilizing search engine optimization (SEO). • Discover a selection of lucrative affiliate products and services, generate sales pages dedicated to these offerings, and subsequently "introduce" them through your website using email campaigns and teasers to generate excitement. To ascertain the most prosperous products, subsequently direct additional traffic to this destination via compensated advertisement. • Identify the most prosperous products and subsequently drive additional traffic to this location via paid promotional campaigns.

You have now acquired the capacity to generate passive income, irrespective of your personal activities, and as you experiment with various techniques, your sales strategy will progressively amplify in effectiveness.

What is the operational mechanism of Affiliate Marketing?

The initial stage in establishing oneself as an affiliate is the identification of a product to market. One can opt to search for products or services on individual websites such as SEO Press or SEMrush, or explore affiliate product marketplace platforms such as Amazon Associates, CJ, ShareASale, ClickBank, among various others.

Subsequently, you proceed to enroll in the product or service in order to acquire a referral link, which is an exclusive identification code allotted to each affiliate upon registration. Ultimately, you will engage in marketing activities and derive financial gains from each successful sale that results from your referral links.

What are your responsibilities as an affiliate marketer?

In the role of an affiliate marketer, your primary responsibility entails:

• Identify superior and more pertinent products to promote.
• Seeking potential clientele through diverse channels such as search engines, social media platforms, paid advertisements, email databases, and more.
• Produce content that holds practical value (such as informative analyses, downloadable guides, instructional

videos, empirical studies, and persuasive web pages)."

• Generate revenue. • Achieve profitability. • Attain financial gains. • Earn a return on investment.

First and foremost, it is paramount that as an affiliate marketer, your primary obligation is to enhance the well-being of individuals by advocating for worthwhile products that aid your specific target group in comprehending their requirements.

Advantages and Disadvantages of Affiliate Marketing:

Affiliate marketing, akin to any other endeavor, possesses both advantages and disadvantages.

Herein lie the chief merits and demerits of affiliate marketing.

Affiliate Marketing Pros

Entry is not difficult. Commencing affiliate marketing is a straightforward endeavor and entails a modest financial investment. The majority of affiliate programs can be joined without any financial obligations, and you will not be required to handle the development, stocking, or shipping of products. Consequently, you will experience a reduced level of burden and accountability.

- Minimal risk. Since you do not possess ownership of the product, there is no risk of incurring any losses in the event that a potential buyer decides not to make a purchase.
- The potential to generate income through passive means. Affiliate marketing holds the capacity to serve as a passive income stream.
- Increased autonomy. Once you begin generating passive income, you will have the flexibility to determine your working hours and location, provided you have internet connectivity.

121

Affiliate Marketing Cons

This will not provide an expedient solution. Generating substantial income often requires a considerable investment of time, effort, and patience in order to cultivate a sizable volume of traffic.

• There is a reduced level of control. As you do not possess ownership or managerial control over the product/service you are recommending, your ability to influence its quality or influence the customer experience is limited.

• Contest. If your affiliate program is appealing, it is possible that you may encounter competition from others in acquiring clients.

There exists variation among affiliate programmes. Although the majority of affiliate commission companies demonstrate trustworthiness and ethical practices, there exist a minority that do not meet these standards. Consequently, there is a possibility that some of these entities might not fulfill their payment obligations as promised. It is imperative to complete your assignments.

Alternative Pricing Structures in Affiliate Marketing

When making a choice regarding an affiliate offer, there are several factors that ought to be taken into account. Various elements such as the originator of the program, payout structure, advertisement format, and authorized sources of traffic, collectively influence the level of success achieved by your campaign.

The pricing model, conversely, will aid you in evaluating the optimal formats, geographies, and other elements of the campaign. Affiliate marketing programs generally operate on a performance-based framework, although there exist a range of pricing models to consider, including pay-per-sale, pay-per-lead, pay-per-click, and revenue sharing, among others.

Pay-Per-Sale

Postscript, commonly known as pay-per-sale (PPS), operates as a pricing framework wherein affiliates must generate sales to receive a corresponding commission. Postscript offers, arguably one of the most time-honored pricing strategies, is typically devised by publishers for moderately priced merchandise due to consumers' heightened inclination towards online purchases of such items. Nevertheless, it is possible for you to manage fashion merchandise and other expensive items that have relatively lower sales rates but offer substantial individual commissions.

Due to the fact that PPS offers are customarily intended for promotion through more straightforward methods, do not feel hesitant to generate content that focuses primarily on the product, with the aim of convincing users to make a purchase. In order to maintain customer engagement, it is imperative to exhibit your distinct personality and deliver valuable content.

Pay-Per-Lead

The pay-per-lead model, also known as PPL, pertains to a pricing structure wherein affiliates receive compensation for each individual who supplies their contact details and converts into a potential lead. Although the process of gathering leads may be simpler compared to the act of making sales, consistently persuading consumers to provide their contact information can present a formidable challenge.

It is important to bear in mind that while PPL offers a lower cost per conversion, accumulating a sufficient number of leads can yield the same monetary returns as PPS. Kindly bear in mind that the offer will delineate the requisite information for registering a conversion. Thus, it is imperative to ensure that you procure all the aforementioned information stipulated in the programme specifics.

Pay-Per-Click

In the domain of digital marketing, the pay-per-click (PPC) model prevails as a widely adopted pricing mechanism. In simpler terms, affiliates are solely responsible for generating clicks and driving traffic to the advertiser's offer page through pay-per-click (PPC) offers.

The primary objective of PPC is to enhance visitor engagement, consequently, advertisers are not obligated to promote a particular product or promotion. On the contrary, these enterprises find great satisfaction in augmenting the volume of visitors directed to their online platforms, thereby allowing you to generate revenue by effectively expanding their web traffic and fulfilling the stipulations of their promotional offerings.

PPC campaigns demonstrate the highest ease of conversion among the listed options; nevertheless, it is crucial to note that they also exhibit the lowest average payouts.

Revenue Share

The purpose of revenue share offerings, also referred to as rev share, is to solicit subscriptions and allocate a portion of the earnings from each client to affiliates. Revenue sharing offers generally extend for the entirety of a client's membership; however, the specific duration may vary depending on the program.

Revenue-sharing agreements are commonly observed within established enterprises and burgeoning brands. These options present an excellent opportunity for experienced affiliates aiming to complement their passive income strategies; however, they generally entail a lengthier conversion process.

Affiliate Marketing Terminologies

Below, we present a compilation of frequently utilized phrases in the domain of affiliate marketing:

Affiliates: Individuals who participate in our affiliate program by promoting and selling products through designated affiliate links.

Affiliate marketplaces such as Shareasale, CJ, and Clickbank represent a few examples of smaller markets in this industry. These function as centralized platforms for affiliate programs across diverse niches.

Affiliate software enables companies to establish an affiliate program that promotes their products.

Associated Identification: Several affiliate networks provide a distinctive identification code which can be integrated onto any webpage of the product site, much like the affiliate hyperlink.

Associate link: Your associate program might furnish you with a unique tracking URL to monitor the advancement of your associate promotion.

Affiliate Manager/OPM: Numerous corporations enlist dedicated affiliate managers to aid publishers in maximizing their earnings through the provision of optimization recommendations.

Method of payment: Numerous affiliate programs provide a diverse range of payout methods.

For instance: Payment methods including cheques, wire transfers, PayPal, and various alternative options.

Percentage/Amount of Commission: The remuneration (or proportion) of affiliate earnings allocated to you for each transaction.

Landing pages serve as distinctive websites designed exclusively for product sales or demos, aimed at enhancing sales performance. The majority of the programs you will be promoting will feature several landing pages, and you can employ A/B testing to assess which ones yield the highest conversion rates.

Two-tier affiliate marketing: This presents an exceptional opportunity to generate revenue through an affiliate program. You get a commission when a sub-affiliate makes a sale via this method, as you suggest others to join affiliate networks (similar to MLM or multi-level marketing). A sub-affiliate commission refers to this variant of income.

Tailored affiliate earnings/account: Numerous establishments provide personalized affiliate remuneration to clients who generate the highest number of affiliate sales on their behalf, as a substitute for a standard affiliate account.

Regarding link clocking, it is evident that a significant proportion of affiliate tracking URLs exhibit subpar quality. One can transform unsightly links into easily comprehensible ones through the utilization of a link obfuscation technique such as URL shorteners or Thirsty Affiliates.

Tailored vouchers: Several affiliate platforms offer the feature of generating customized discounts, which can effectively track and analyze sales. In addition, the utilization of personalized discount vouchers has the potential to enhance affiliate sales for your business.

This method represents an exceptional avenue for companies offering an affiliate program to generate complimentary publicity while economizing on advertising expenditures.

When encountering coupons or discount links, it is frequently the case that these links are affiliate links, whereby webmasters stand to gain profit upon your purchase.

Each affiliate programme is governed by its own unique set of terms and conditions.

As an illustration, stipulations regarding payments, policies relating to cookies, and similar matters.

Allow me to elucidate the matter concerning the cookie policy, as it pertains to a subject of moderate significance, that may facilitate your comprehension of the potentialities within affiliate marketing.

Numerous affiliate products offer a cookie duration ranging from 30 to 150 days. This signifies that upon a visitor's initial click on your affiliate link leading to an affiliate product, you will obtain an affiliate commission even if they do not make an immediate purchase. Instead, if they revisit the site within the subsequent 30 to 150 days and complete a transaction, you will still be eligible for the commission.

Selection of Affiliate Programs - Which Option Is Most Suitable?

Inquire about any queries prior to enrolling in the affiliate program. Conduct thorough investigation into the program choices you aim to engage with. Get some answers. As it will constitute a pivotal juncture determining your future accomplishments.

Is it not financially burdensome to participate? The vast majority of affiliate programs currently available are provided at no cost. What is your rationale for expressing satisfaction with individuals requesting a small fee prior to your enrollment? When are tax disbursements scheduled to be issued? Every program is different. Certain occurrences happen on a variety of intervals, including monthly, quarterly, and so forth. Select a cheque that aligns with your preferred payment timeframe. The majority of affiliate programs establish a prescribed threshold which affiliates are required to reach or surpass for the issuance of a monetary remittance.

What percentage of your sales result in success? The mean value of the required number of impressions for a banner or text link to successfully drive sales, as inferred from comprehensive affiliate metrics. This factor holds significant importance as it elucidates the amount of traffic required to attain the sales commission. How is the tracking of referrals from affiliate sites conducted and how long is the storage duration for such data in the system? In order to monitor and trace the sources of traffic to your website, it is essential to place reliance on your tracking system. This singular method represents the sole means by which your sales can be duly acknowledged. The duration of these individuals' stay within the system holds significant importance as well. This phenomenon arises due to the potential occurrence that certain visitors may not engage in an immediate purchasing decision, but instead exhibit an inclination to revisit at a later time with the intention of making a purchase. Determine the possibility of still attaining credit for sales beyond a specified date. What variety of affiliate statistics are accessible? The chosen affiliate program must offer comprehensive statistical data. If you opt to view it, it ought to be accessible on the internet. Regularly monitoring your personal statistics is crucial in gauging the number of impressions, views, and sales your website has contributed.

Impressions refer to the frequency with which a visitor encounters a banner or text link on your website. Views consist of individuals who engage by clicking on a banner or text link. Are affiliate programs remunerated for both views, impressions, and sales commissions? Additionally, it is crucial to make payments as impressions and views play a significant role in generating income from sales commissions. This holds particular significance if the program you are utilizing provides a diminished level of profit to fulfill this benchmark.

May I inquire as to the identity of the online merchant? It is imperative to ascertain the identity and background of the business entity, in order to ensure the establishment of a reputable and reliable corporate association. They possess a comprehensive understanding of the merchandise they retail and the mean volume they generate. Having a comprehensive understanding of the providers offering affiliate programs will facilitate the process of discerning whether or not the program is truly suitable for both your website and yourself.

Could you please clarify whether the partnership is structured as a one-tier or two-tier program? Graduated programs solely compensate for the clientele that you establish. A dual-level program entails covering both the company's expenses and compensating the affiliates who are sponsored through your program. Some affiliate programs offer a modest remuneration for each newly referred affiliate. such as rent. What was the most recent tax payment made? A considerable percentage ranging from 20% to 80% (in certain instances, even up to 100%) constitutes a fee that is typically remunerated by numerous programs. The payment for each access ranges from 0.01% to 0.05%. If an opportunity arises where you encounter a program that compensates for impression-based advertising, the expenditure involved is minimal. Based on the statistical evidence provided, it is evident that you now grasp the significance of the average sales value and sales ratio. Herein lies a limited selection of inquiries that you ought to address prior to enlisting in the affiliate program. Prior to integrating the program onto your website, it is imperative that you acquaint yourself with key facets of your selected software. Please attempt the subsequent inquiries pertaining to the selection of an affiliate program. This will assist you in selecting the appropriate program for your website among the myriad of programs at your disposal.

Considerations for Selecting Networks
Numerous accounts of distressing experiences regarding affiliate programs and networks abound. The information

was consistently disseminated, resulting in apprehension among certain individuals who were hesitant to participate. The narrative they were acquainted with could potentially be identical.

In summary, within such a market, the absence of genuine and reputable products is attributable to the presence of illicit practices such as illegal programs or pyramid schemes. You would prefer not to be affiliated with these fraudulent endeavors. Undoubtedly, you seek to align yourself with a program that offers products of utmost quality which you wholeheartedly endorse. The increasing number of individuals who have successfully enrolled demonstrates the existence of reputable affiliate programs that can be relied upon.

What are the reasons for engaging in an affiliate program?

It provides you with the opportunity to engage in part-time employment. This will enable you to enjoy a substantial passive income. And thus, it is by virtue of this fact that you possess the qualities and responsibilities characteristic of a proprietor of a modest-sized enterprise. Numerous individuals have achieved significant wealth as a result of engaging in affiliate programs. They serve as living evidence of the arduousness of the work. Persisting in the pursuit of knowledge, inspiring and coaching others will yield positive results.

Should you choose to enlist, it is important to bear in mind that you will be embarking upon a pursuit that aligns with your abilities. In this manner, you are able to employ any means necessary to achieve success.

What are the criteria for selecting a high-quality affiliate program for advertising? "Prior to making a selection, it would be prudent to take into account the following suggestion:

The programs that are of your interest and hold significance to you.

Purchasing the product yourself is a highly effective method to ensure that it aligns with the type of program you intend to endorse. Should this be the case, it is plausible that a considerable number of individuals would display interest in these aforementioned programs and products. Find high quality programs. For instance, locate individuals who possess extensive connections with numerous authorities within their respective domains. This will afford you the opportunity to assess the quality benchmarks of the programs you are enrolled in. Collaborate with individuals who produce tangible and effective outputs.

May I inquire about the source of your knowledge? Please conduct preliminary research on the subject matter. If feasible, endeavor to identify a select group of individuals who can vouch for the credibility of the program, comprising both members and customers. This program caters to an expanding demographic.

This fosters a perpetually increasing demand for your referrals. Note that. There are online platforms and discourse opportunities available for your active engagement, where you can obtain valuable and reliable feedback. Optimal selections would consist of income programs that offer residual earnings and compensation structures which allocate 40% or higher proportions of payouts. Certain programs provide this kind of incentive. Find one carefully. Do not expend your valuable time on programs that fail to adequately recognize and compensate for your diligent efforts. Please be cognizant of the minimal threshold to achieve a share, or a sales objective that is exceedingly arduous to attain.

Certain affiliate programs impose certain prerequisites that need to be met in order to qualify for commission disbursement. Please ensure that you are able to meet their specified requirements.

Select a comprehensive toolkit equipped with abundant resources and utilities to expedite the growth of your business. These features are not present in every affiliate program. Utilize it and select an option equipped with a plethora of functional tools for employment. Ensure that your program possesses a validated framework to effectively oversee both network operations and financial transactions.

Additionally, ensure that it is accessible on the internet to facilitate convenient and unrestricted verification at any given time and location. A program that provides members with a compelling motivation to renew their membership on each occasion.

Affiliate programs that provide continuous support and regular product updates have a higher tendency to maintain their membership base. These elements have the potential to expand your network.

Discern the program options that members have an aversion towards. In a comparable manner, you may examine the discourse forum. If you are acquainted with an individual possessing that particular program, it is perfectly acceptable to inquire whether there are prevalent limitations associated with it. You possess a profound and concentrated understanding of the affiliate programs and networks that you endorse. Having knowledge about the program you are entering can assist in predicting and mitigating potential issues moving forward.

Effortless Gains Through Utilizing Pay-Per-Click in Your Business

Pay-per-click (PPC) is considered one of the primary classifications among the four predominant categories of search engines. PPC is also regarded as a highly efficient and cost-efficient method of targeted online advertising. Per Forbes' analysis, the annual value of PPC, which stands for Pay Per Click, amounts to $2 billion, with projections indicating a substantial increase to nearly $8 billion by 2008.

Let us examine the mechanics of pay-per-click advertising on search engines. These search engines generate directories and evaluate the directories by considering the monetary bid offered by website proprietors for every click on the respective search engine. Advertisers engage in a competitive process of bidding against one another in order to obtain higher rankings for specific keywords or phrases. The bidder who offers the highest amount for a specific keyword or phrase attains the top position on the website's PPC search engine, while the bidders with the second and third highest bids for the same keyword or phrase are positioned below.

Based on the amount you choose to bid per click, your advertisement will effectively distinguish itself on the results page. What strategies can be employed to generate income through the utilization of Pay-Per-Click advertising within the realm of affiliate marketing?

The majority of affiliate programs solely remunerate upon the completion of a purchase or delivery subsequent to a visitor's redirection to your website. Variations in your website content and the demographic of your traffic can result in fluctuating revenue.

The inclusion of PPC in affiliate marketing programs is justified by its inherent ability to generate higher earnings in comparison to non-PPC based affiliate programs. In this manner, you have the opportunity to generate income through the clicks generated by your website visitors. In contrast to certain programs, remuneration is not provided for sales or advertising efforts. PPC can prove to be highly advantageous for your website. PPC is seamlessly integrated with search engine platforms. Affiliate programs offer the opportunity to captivate individuals who may not manifest an initial interest in your product or service. Individuals who discontinue their usage of the platform without returning. In addition to generating commissions through individuals who conduct online searches and come across the desired products and services, your website is also acknowledged as a highly valuable asset. Prospective visitors who successfully locate the information they require on your website are inclined to return and delve deeper into the offerings and content you have available. Subsequently, they return to the Internet in search of alternative merchandise. This particular affiliate program offers a convenient avenue to generate supplementary revenue. As an illustration, in the event that a user accesses your website and initiates a pay-per-click search engine inquiry, subsequently selecting an advertiser-furnished listing, the advertiser's account shall undergo a deduction of funds for the corresponding click. His

In consideration of this, a remuneration of 30% - 80% of the advertiser's offer shall be accorded to you.

PPC serves a strategic purpose beyond generating revenue. Additionally, it aids in the promotion of your own website. The commissions acquired through the majority of programs are eligible for immediate use, without any prerequisite of minimum advertising revenue. This method ranks among the most efficient means of converting initial website visitors into focused individuals who are inclined to make purchases of your products and services. What would be the impact if I were to incorporate PPC into my affiliate program?

PPC platforms typically offer a range of pre-designed affiliate tools that can be seamlessly integrated into your website. The search bar, banners, text links, and select 404 error pages are among the tools frequently employed. Several search engines utilize proprietary solutions and potentially provide affiliate programs under a white label arrangement. By incorporating a few lines of code, you have the ability to seamlessly integrate a co-branded search engine hosted remotely onto your website.

What are the primary benefits associated with this? An increased amount of funds, as opposed to an increased quantity of funds. Additionally, an opportunity to generate enduring commissions presents itself when you refer your acquaintances in the field of web development to the platform. Think about this. From where can one acquire such benefits while generating revenue through their website? It is advantageous to invest time in acquiring knowledge about practical tools that can enhance your affiliate program. Instead, it serves as a financial opportunity in and of itself. We strongly advise that you familiarize yourself with the intricacies of utilizing search engine PPC within your affiliate program, as failing to do so may result in missed opportunities for increased earnings.

Implementing Recommended Product Strategies to Enhance Profitability

There are numerous strategies available to enhance one's earnings and uphold the integrity of one's affiliate marketing account. Acquiring various skills and strategies is a straightforward endeavor. There is no necessity to travel elsewhere. Accessible round the clock, every day of the week, through online platforms. One of the primary methods for enhancing outcomes and boosting sales in the field of affiliate marketing is the strategic promotion of products. Numerous marketing professionals are cognizant of the fact that this method is highly efficacious in advertising a specific product. If one garners sufficient trust from their customers or visitors, they will find that their referrals are also trusted.

Nevertheless, it is imperative to exercise utmost caution when employing this approach. When one begins to endorse something as a point of reference, it compromises one's credibility. This holds particularly true in cases where the offer appears inflated and ill-suited. Do not hesitate to engage in discussions pertaining to a particular product or service. Rather than incurring a deduction of points, your proposal possesses a greater level of accuracy and trustworthiness. If your visitors possess a sincere inclination towards your offerings, they will readily embrace acquiring knowledge about the advantages and disadvantages of your product, as well as its application. When offering a suggestion for a specific product, it is crucial to bear in mind certain key points in order to enhance effectiveness and maximize personal benefit. Regard yourself as a bona fide authority in your respective field. Remember this simple formula. Confidence is inversely proportional to the level of price resistance. If your visitors perceive you as a knowledgeable authority in your specific field and have confidence in your expertise, it is highly probable that they will proceed with the intended purchase.

Conversely, should you fail to demonstrate trust and confidence in your product recommendations, individuals will reciprocate these sentiments, leading them to seek alternative products or services from sources they deem trustworthy. What is your perception of this particular experience? We provide unparalleled and groundbreaking solutions that are not accessible elsewhere. Demonstrate the efficacy of the product/service being advocated in accordance with its stated claims. Naturally, we consistently receive outstanding feedback and endorsements from prominent figures in the industry. Exercise utmost caution in order to prevent the emergence of fear. It is more desirable to remain composed and self-assured rather than raise one's voice and draw undue notice. Furthermore, would you desire to project an unprofessional image and create confusion among potential clients and customers? It is most advisable to maintain a composed and self-assured demeanor simultaneously. And remember. Perspective is not stupid. They possess considerable expertise and will be fully knowledgeable in all aspects relevant to your needs. If they substantiate their claims with concrete evidence and factual data, they will demonstrate a readiness to allocate significant financial resources towards advertising efforts. But if not, they are smart enough to look at their competitors and see what they have to offer. Additionally, it is crucial to provide complimentary promotional materials during the promotion of your product. For a considerable duration, individuals have become accustomed to the notion of distributing complimentary items as a means to augment their earnings. Only a minority of individuals engage in this practice to endorse affiliate products. Promote your product or service or offer a complimentary estimate accompanied by relevant details. It is advisable to conduct thorough testing and evaluate the performance of your product and support prior to implementing product recommendations. Do not engage in the promotion of unnecessary products and services, as it poses a risk. Consider the significant amount of time that was invested in establishing trust with your visitors. A significant error has occurred. Provide products that are consistently reliable to the fullest extent possible. If you encounter unexpected difficulties, please consult the support documentation for your product to avoid any confusion among those seeking assistance. Please examine the affiliate market and evaluate the available strategies. You might overlook the offers provided by the product. On occasion, the efficacy of your program is not solely reliant on your action plan. Be among the select few individuals who dare to test and validate the value of your product offering.

Printed in the USA
CPSIA information can be obtained
at www.ICGtesting.com
LVHW020825210923
758625LV00014B/821

9 781837 876846